ROB HERWIG

# 128 HOUSEPLANTS MORE
# YOU CAN GROW

With color photographs of each,
plus 12 black-and-white photographs

Collier Books, New York, New York

All photographs by Rob Herwig

**COLLIER BOOKS**
*A Division of Macmillan Publishing Co., Inc.*
NEW YORK

**COLLIER MACMILLAN PUBLISHERS**
LONDON

Macmillan Publishing Co, Inc.
866 Third Avenue, New York, N.Y. 10022

Collier — Macmillan Canada Ltd.

LIbrary of Congress Catalog Card Number: 73-18766

First Collier Books Edition 1974

Printed in the Netherlands

# Preface

This book is a continuation of *128 Houseplants You Can Grow,* which enjoyed great success. However, it dealt only with the 128 most popular plants, some as groups. Now I have selected an additional 130 plants that are often grown in private houses, offices, and public places.

Indoors, houseplants give us back a little bit of the nature that we miss so sadly in cities. As people began to recognize this dificiency, houseplants became more popular. This is a good thing in my opinion, especially when the plants are treated as living beings, and not merely as decoration. The increase of the so-called throwaway plants, like pot-chrysanthemums, is not an expedient that stimulates a love of plants. More satisfaction is obtained from a friend's gift of a simple cutting which will grow and live for many years.

In this book, I have maintained the same system of symbols used in *128 Houseplants.* They have proved to be very efficient and are especially helpful when you take the trouble to learn them by heart before you start using the book. They also facilitate the comparison of growing conditions for different plants. You'll find the explanation of the symbols on pages 4—9 and, in briefer form, on the inside front cover. Happy growing!

*Rob Herwig*

# Light

Sufficient light is very important to the good health of your houseplants. Plants are often placed too far from the light — in the middle of the room — and most plants aren't very happy with this treatment. There is less light even one yard from the window than there is on the windowsill, as you can measure for yourself with a light meter (*photo, upper left*). Some plants can be given too much light; full sun can be damaging. It may be best to have venetian blinds on your windows so that you can adjust the amount of light yourself (*photo, upper right*).

In this book, each plant is given one or more light symbols. You can immediately tell where it is best to place your plants. The symbols and their meanings are as follows:

☼ **Likes full sun if possible.** Have no curtains or blinds between the window and the plant.

◑ **Likes moderate daylight.** If you place this plant in front of a window with southern exposure, have a curtain or blind between the window and the plant between 10 and 4 on sunny days. Windows facing east and west do not need this screening.

● **Can stand a rather dark location.** This can vary from a tree-shaded window to a spot a few yards from a light window.

# Temperature

Tropical plants require a high temperature thoughout the year. Succulents, cacti, and many other plants like warmth in summer but moderate coolness in winter. In modern dwellings this can often be a problem, but you should try to find a solution. Plants flourish much better at the proper (or natural) temperature. The photos opposite show a box of cacti in their summer location (a cool garage) and in their winter location (the house). The desired summer temperature is shown in this book by the following symbols:

| **Warm.** Minimum 60–65° F.; with sufficient light, the temperature may reach 85° F. During a rest period the temperature can be lower.

| **Medium.** Minimum 50–55° F.; maximum 65–70° F., if care is given to provide adequate ventilation.

| **Cold.** Minimum 40–45° F. at night; maximum 55–60° F. The plants need fresh air and in the summer are at their best outdoors.

# Water

It's impossible to say exactly how much water a plant needs. That usually depends on the temperature of the room, the kind of pot (earthenware or plastic), and the size of the plant. The best way to determine how much moisture is in the earth is to touch it with your finger (*photo, left*). Usually, you should avoid letting the pot stand in a saucer filled with water (*photo, right*), because then the soil will become too wet. The plant that is the best-known exception to this is the Cyperus. Because tap water can be very hard and sometimes contains dangerous salts, rainwater is often used. If the rainwater is polluted, use tap water purified by running it through a special filter. The ordinary household water softeners, based on a change in ions, offer no improvement.

The symbols and their meanings are as follows:

 **Likes a lot of water at a time** and is happy with regular dunkings. The pots, however, must not stand in saucers filled with water. Don't let the soil dry out completely between waterings.

 **Keep moderately damp.** Don't give too much water at one time but give it regularly. Test the dampness often with your finger. Dunking is seldom or never necessary.

 **Requires little water.** These plants (the succulents) are all able to absorb moisture through their stalks, tubers, or leaves. They can go without water for several days, and the soil can become completely dry between waterings.

# Humidity

In most rooms the air is too dry for houseplants. Many beautiful plants which look lovely at the nursery or florist shop can be kept alive only a short time at home. Spraying with water is often a help (*photo, left*), as are an electric humidifier (*photo, right*), providing a wide windowsill (less direct dry air), or, especially, an enclosed flower window. The desirable humidity is shown in this book by the following symbols:

**Needs a high humidity,** which is difficult to provide in a heated room in the winter. This is really a greenhouse plant but can be successfully kept in the home during the summer.

**Needs moderate humidity.** The plant will do well in most rooms, even when there is central heating, provided it is sprayed often and isn't allowed to stand in too dry a draft.

**Accepts dry air** very well. Suitable for very dry, unfavorable locations.

# Soil

Many plants grow very well in the readily available, prepackaged nursery soil; but for those plants that strongly favor an acid or alkaline soil, you will do better to mix the soil yourself. The photo on the left shows the ingredients for a very acid growing medium: prepackaged soil and peat moss. Use about half of each. On the right you see how to mix a more alkaline, lighter mixture. The prepackaged soil is combined with 30 percent sand and, for each pound of the mixture, about $\frac{1}{2}$ ounce of lime is added. Both mixtures should be thoroughly stirred.

Experienced gardeners also achieve success by adding loam, leaf meal, compost, and the like to their plant mixtures.

Orchids, and some bromeliads, which in a natural state grow on trees, desire or even require a very special mixture, to which fernroots or spagnum moss is added. Details will be given in the individual texts.

# Repotting

**A**    **Requires acid soil.** The use of a packaged houseplant soil, with a pH (ratio of acid to alkaline) of 4 to 5, is fine.

**K**    **Requires a loamy soil.** Mix ordinary houseplant soil with some extra lime and sand or use a special mixture containing clay or loam.

**L**    **Requires a very light, acid soil.** This applies to orchids, bromeliads, and similar plants. See the explanation in the text.

Not only are the minerals in the soil of a potted plant quickly exhausted, but the soil itself often gets polluted with harmful salts from tap water, an over supply of certain fertilizers, and other chemicals. Therefore, most plants should be repotted every year, preferably in the spring. Only very old or very slow-growing plants can continue to survive in the same soil. For the plants that need a damp soil (see the symbols), I advise a plastic pot. In other cases, clay pots are more practical, because too much water often accumulates in plastic pots. Any pot you use must have a hole in the bottom so that any excess water can run out.

To repot a plant, slip it out of the old flowerpot by holding it upside down (*photo, left*). If it doesn't come out, break the pot. Now take a somewhat larger pot, and over the hole at the bottom, place a piece of broken pot. Working carefully so as to do as little damage as possible to the roots, lightly knead the old soil clump so that most of the old earth falls off. Then put a little of the new soil in the bottom of the pot, set the plant on top, and pack more new soil around it. When the plant is firmly in place, sprinkle a thin layer of new earth on top of the soil already in the pot. For easy watering there should be $\frac{1}{2}-\frac{3}{4}$ inch between the soil and the top of the pot. After repotting, it's a good idea to prune a little of the top part of the plant to minimize surface evaporation. Keep the repotted plant out of the sun for a few weeks.

# Acalypha (Foxtail, Copper Leaf) ▶   ☼ ❗ ◊◊◖ 🇰

Very showy houseplants, but in most cases you will not be able to keep them long. The species *A. hispida* (pictured), which has long red foxtails, is specially fragile. It is fond of moist air, and will die in winter if kept in dry, overheated rooms. If you like, try to make cuttings in November–December.

The Copper Leaf, *A.wilkesiana,* does not grow long tails but has nicely colored leaves. 'Musaica' has a bronze fond with red, pink, and orange spots; and Marginata has a lighter edge and red veins. The Copper Leaf can be propagated from cuttings, too.

*PUŠKVOREC*

# Acorus   *Acorus calamus*
# (Dwarf Japanese Sweet flag) ▶▶   ☼ ❗ ◊◊◊◖ 🇰

Striped varieties of this pretty, hardy garden perennial are sometimes used for indoor decorations. The correct Latin name for the plant illustrated is *Acorus gramineus* 'Variegatus'. The leaves are striped green and white. When it is green and gold, we should call it Aureovariegatus.

The Sweet flag is a marsh plant and should be kept in clayish soil, always moist. It prefers moderate temperatures. Multiplying is accomplished easily by dividing the roots.

# Aechmea ▶   ☼ ❗ ◊◊◖ ＼ 🇱

**The Aechmea,** originally grown in Brazil, is one of the most popular bromeliads for indoors. The plants have an interesting, tropical appearance and beautiful flowers. Alas, the flower appears only once and the plant dies after flowering. But it always produces at least one baby plant from its base. When it is about half the size of its mother, you can cut off the new plant with a sharp knife, saving some of the roots. It may flower within two or three years.

Very well known is *Aechmea fasciata,* Silver Vase. Its big, broad flower stand is pink, with ovoid, bluish flowers nestled in it. Pictured also is the popular *A. fulgens var. discolor* (Purple Coral Berry) with a much higher flower stem and beautifully colored leaves.

# Aeonium (Saucer Plant) ▶▶   ☼ ❗ ◊＼ 🇰

These succulent plants of different shapes are very easy to keep. One of the most spectacular species is *Aeonium tabulaeforme,* Saucer Plant (pictured), which forms a very flat rosette, consisting of about 100–200 leaves. After having flowered, the plant dies and propagating can only be done from seed or leaf cuttings. *A. arboreum* forms loose rosettes on the tops of woody stems. Leaves drop in winter. There are many more species which you can grow. Like all succulents, these like a hot, sunny place in summer and a cool, practically dry one in winter. In southern zones you may keep them in the open.

Most species can be propagated from cuttings, also from seed.

# Aeschynanthus (Basket Vines) ▶

Nearly all species of *Aeschynanthus* are epiphytes and live on trees in Indonesia and Asia. Indoors you can cultivate these plants on a piece of fern root or peat. Pots should be filled with a mixture of peat, leaf mold, and well-rotted manure. During winter give less water, but keep in a heated room.

*A. marmoratus* has leaves spotted dark and light green. *A. pulcher*, with drooping twigs, has red flowers in the summer. Always impressive is *A. speciosus* (pictured) with orange red flowers, up to 3 inches long, with the stamen running out of the flower.

Propagating can be done under plastic, but extra warmth is needed.

*KLANOKVĚT*

# Agapanthus (African Lily) ▶▶

The wonderful blue African Lily is very hardy in southern regions where it is easily grown as a border perennial. In the north, however, it is better suited as a tub plant, which stays outside in summer and in winter has a beauty sleep in the cool greenhouse, where 39°–47° F. is maintained.

All this fun can start with a small potted *A. umbellatus* (pictured), which you can obtain from a florist or garden center. It grows bigger every year and eventually will require a rather large tub, because there are lots of roots, giving a great many flowers. Repotting, however, should be done only when the plant is literally bursting out of its pot.

Propagation is via seed.

# Agave (Century Plant) ▶

This is a real plant of the Americas from the heart of Mexico. Indeed, the Latin name of one species is *A. americana*.

Pictured is a small specimen of the striped variety, called 'Marginata'. Of course, there are many other *Agavae*, for instance *A. victoriae-reginae*, which is white edged and forms a small rosette. In the south your *Agave* can grow outside and stay there in the winter. But where frost can be expected, you should give it a sheltered and light place in the house, or better the greenhouse. In this season little water is required. In the summer you can place small plants on the windowsill, but bigger ones grow better in tubs in a sunny place outside.

Propagation from seed.

*NESTAŘEC*

# Ageratum (Ageratum) ▶▶

The use of *Ageratum houstonianum* as a potted plant is limited to one season. It is an annual, commonly used as a bedding plant outdoors. In a pot, it flowers beautifully before a bright window, especially when you give it plenty of water and food. At the end of the season you can either throw the plant away or keep it through the winter. In most cases you will get nicer plants when you take cuttings in early spring and these need extra warmth.

# Aglaonema (Chinese Evergreen) ▶ ☼ 🌡 ◊◊◊🍃 **L**

There are numerous species of this very strong foliage plant, most of which have oblong, white-painted, green leaves. They are suitable for decorations, together with other leaf plants.

Very common is *A. costatum,* with spreading growth and dark green, white spotted, shiny leaves. White Rajah Evergreen, *A. commutatum,* with silver-marked foliage grows much higher. The form 'Albovariegatum' is pictured. *A. roebelinii* makes leaves up to 12 inches long which are green with silver markings. *A. oblongifolium* 'Curtisii' is very hardy, has the same size, and is white along the veins. Propagating is done by cuttings which must be kept warm and by seed.

# Allamanda (Golden Trumpet) ▶▶ ☼ 🌡 ◊◊🍃 **K**

Silent, golden trumpet flowers make this fast-growing climber especially outstanding in a nice warm greenhouse with humid conditions. The best-known species is *Allamanda cathartica*. For use as a potted-plant, however, the variety *grandiflora* (pictured) is usually preferred. The Golden Trumpet is very fond of some additional nutrients in the summer. Cut the plant back considerably in November, because young shoots will give more blooms. Winter temperature should be 65° F., and watering should be reduced. Propagating from young shoots, which root at 78° F. under plastic.

# Ampelopsis (Porcelain Ampelopsis) ▶☼ 🌡 ◊◊🍃 **K**

If you are fond of Latin names, here's a beautiful one for you: *Ampelopsis brevipedunculata* 'Elegans'.

It is a nice, fast climber for cool rooms, it can even grow outside and stay there in frost-free winters. In a hot, dry room it will fade away and lose its leaves.

If your plant has these symptoms, you can easily save it by taking cuttings from the top of the shoots. They will root in a mixture of peat and sand, with a temperature of about 68° F.

# Ananas (Pineapple) ▶▶ ☼ 🌡 ◊◊◊ ◊◊🍃 **A**

Pictured is *Ananas comosus* 'Variegatus', a variegated form of the same pineapple that is commercially grown for its fruit.

The leaves have white lines along the outside and are sometimes a little flushed. This decorative form also produces a little pineapple, but it is hardly edible. If you leave the fruit growing (and why shouldn't you?) it will produce a bunch of leaves on top, as is clearly visible in the picture (the fruit is underneath).

Winter temperature should not fall below 60° F.

# Ardisia (Coral Berry) ▶

*Ardisia crispa* is an interesting green-leaved houseplant which is mainly available in the fall when its red berries are present. The berries last for a very long time, sometimes until the flowers appear the following spring. You can see this feature in the photograph.

In order to keep your Coral Berry fresh, temperature should not be too warm in the winter and the air must be sufficiently moist. Repot in the spring and wait for the new flowers. Then on the flower pistels pread the pollen with a small brush in order to get many berries.

Progapagated by seed and cuttings in a warm medium.

# Astrophytum (Star Cactus) ▶▶

These are decorative cacti with interestingly shaped bodies. Old plants do especially well when placed in adequate pots. In the illustration you can see two young specimens to the right *Astrophytum myriostigma,* commonly called Bishop's Cap, as its shape suggests. The body is spotted with thousands of tiny white dots and is thornless. Flowers are yellow and bloom often. The cactus on the left is called *A. ornatum* or Monk's Hood. Its body is clearly divided by 8 prominent spiral folds and its spines are very distinct.

Like all cacti, *Astrophytum* likes a cool, dry winter (43° F.).

# Aucuba (Aucuba) ▶

This well-known evergreen is a popular garden plant. In America it is hardy from Washington DC Southward. There is a green and a variegated form. The finer variegated types, however, are grown for indoor decoration. They are not quite so hardy, but can withstand some frost. 'Crotonifolia' has beautiful spotted leaves, like those of a *Codiaeum* or Croton. 'Goldiana' shows a yellow center in its leaves and 'Sulphur' is yellow-edged.

When grown indoors, *Aucuba* should be kept as cool as possible, especially in the winter. Propagation can be done from cuttings (with bottom heat) or seed.

# Begonia I ▶▶ KYSALA

In this book I would like to introduce some interesting begonias that are worth growing but are not so commonly known.

Top left is *Begonia heracleifolia,* 'Star Begonia', from Mexico, with its hand-shaped, attractively patterned leaves. To its right *B. corallina* is pictured, a species of which many hybrids are cultivated, some 6 feet high. Flowers are pink or white, culture is easy. *B. foliosa* (bottom left) has very small leaves on overhanging branches and tiny white flowers. At bottom right is *B. boweri,* 'Nigra-Marga' commonly called Stitch-leaf Begonia; a nice species with olive green to dark brown pointed leaves.

# Begonia II ►

Some other fine begonias, are (top left) *B. socotrana,* a parent of the now quite common Lorraine-begonias. At the base it is somewhat tuberous. Top right is *B. masoniana* 'Iron Cross Begonia' a fairly new plant introduced in 1952 by Maurice Mason. Bottom left is *B. imperialis* 'Imperial Begonia', with its velvet leaves, colored bronze brown or sometimes emerald green. It has nice flowers, too. To its right is *B. olsoniae,* a rare species, with spreading growth, dotted leaves, and small white flowers. The foreground shows an ordinary tuberous begonia, also often used as a houseplant.
Propagating is easy by cuttings.

# Billbergia ►►

These are without doubt the strongest *Bromelias* there are. The *Billbergia nutans* or Queen's Tears illustrated is especially indestructible. It is always in flower regardless of its location. There is no need to take the old rosettes away or propagate the baby ones: you will ultimately have a pot full of rosettes, old and new ones at the same time. When the pot becomes too full, repot to give fresh earth and throw old rosettes away.
Another strong species is called *B. x windii,* it has a long, yellow-green flowerstalk, not hanging. *B. x* 'Saundersii-Hybrid' or Rainbow Plant has variegated leaves.

# Browallia (Browallia) ►

Most kinds are annuals, grown for bedding outside, but some are also sold as pot plants. For this purpose we mostly find *Browallia speciosa* (pictured) or the still more compact *B. viscosa* 'Saphir'. The grower sows the seeds in early spring and puts 4 young plants in a pot. Topping is necessary to obtain well-branched plants. Flowers appear from about middle May. They continue to bloom regardless of whether the plant is in a sheltered place outside or in a warm room. In the autumn the plants can be discarded or new plants can be propagated from cuttings.

# Brunfelsia ►►

These nice shrubs can be grown outside, in southern regions. The big violet flowers often fade quickly to white. They have common names such as Yesterday, Today and Tomorrow and Kiss-me-quick. The illustrated species, *Brunfelsia calycina* has flowers that keep their beautiful color for a long time. Main flowering time is January–April. Keep the air as moist as possible if the plant is in a heated room. Give a little rest in May with less water and no food. At that time repot if necessary. You can put the plant in the garden, but avoid full sun. Propagating is difficult because cuttings root very slowly.

# Caladium (Caladium) ▶ VŽOVNÍK

*Caladium* from tropical America is very popular in the United States, especially in the south, where it can be grown outside. In most zones, however, this is a potted plant for the greenhouse or a heated room that is not too dry. *Caladium* forms tuberous roots that can be placed in a pot in January–March. It prefers winter temperatures of 70°–78° F. and porous soil with a lot of peat. In summer it should be kept about 68° F. with bright light, but not in full sunshine. Give plenty of water. In September let the plants dry out until all the leaves fall off and keep the tubers in the pots during winter at a temperature of 64–68° F.

# Calathea (Calathea) ▶▶

A warmth-loving tropical plant that comes to us in many species, most of them very suitable for indoor growing. Pictured is *C. makoyana,* called Peacock Plant. *C. lancifolia* (*syn. C. insignis*) or Rattlesnake Plant, has very long and hard leaves that are yellowish and blotted olive; the reverse side of the leaf is maroon. *C. zebrina* or Zebra Plant, with its large emerald leaves, has a dark brown striped pattern. A light soil with extra peat is best. Use wide pots or let the plants grow free. Propagation by dividing.

# Callistemon (Bottlebrush) ▶

These plants, with interesting flowers resembling a long, narrow bottlebrush come from Australia and Tasmania, where they grow to a height of 10 feet. Flowering time is May or June. A lot of species are known, but most popular as a houseplant is *Callistemon citrinus* (syn. *C. lanceolatus*). The form pictured, 'Splendens', has especially long filaments. The Bottlebrush can be grown outside in summer, preferably in tubs with a mixture of leaf mold, manure, peat, and sand. In the winter a cool greenhouse is best.
Propagating can be done from cuttings that root at a temperature of 64–68° F.

PEPŘOVNÍK
# Capsicum (Christmas Pepper) ▶▶

All edible red pepper is grown on this genus. This plant is selected for its nice looking fruits and is used for indoor growing. The proper name for the houseplant is *C. annuum,* which indicates that it lasts for only one year. Don't confuse this plant with the similar looking Jerusalem cherry (*Solanum pseudocapsicum*), which has round fruit and lasts for many years.
Sowing can be done from February onward, under glass. See that a temperature of about 68–78° F. is maintained. Pick out the young plants, put 3–5 together in each pot and keep in a moist atmosphere a few days before planting them in the open room.

# Cattleya (Cattleya Orchid) ▶▶

The *Cattleya* is a most delightful orchid with big flowers that comes to us in a great many species and hybrids, some of which are fragrant. Cultivation indoors is rather difficult because the plants require moist air, especially in the summer. A greenhouse will always give better results. In the growth period the orchid needs plenty of water, but let the roots get dry between waterings. During the rest period temperatures can be kept as low as 55° F., air can be drier, and watering less frequent. Rest is always given after flowering and after a new growth has developed. For potting, fern root and peat may be used, but orchids can also be grown in bark.

# Carex (Sedge) ▶ OSTRICE

This is a simple, grass-like plant that can be used in greenhouses and rooms that are not too hot. Although this is a member of the *Cyperus* family, the soil should *not* be wet, only constantly moist. The correct name is *Carex brunnera* 'Variegata', but you will also find this plant under other names, for instance, *C. elegantissima*. The best temperature for Sedge is 43–60° F. a centrally heated room may be too hot. Propagating can be done only by division.

# Catharanthus
# (Madagascar Periwinkle) ▶

This little plant is more commonly known under the name *Vinca rosea* and it is an inhabitant of Indonesia. In the south it can be grown outside in a shady place, but sometimes this pretty annual is offered as a potted plant. The flowers which can be violet, red, pink, or white, bloom in summer and fall.
Although plants can be kept in winter and propagated from cuttings, you may just as well grown them from seed. This work starts in February, preferably in a hothouse, but it is possible in a heated room under glass or plastic.

# Cephalocereus (Old Man Cactus) ▶▶

When you visit the greenhouse of a cactus amateur, you will most probably find a lot of these gray-haired cacti. In their natural surroundings, these plants need the hairs as a protection against the deadly hot sun. And indeed the shade underneath is most effective. No doubt the most beautiful of the gray-haired cacti is *Cephalocereus senilis* (pictured). If you look closely, you will notice that the plant is grafted onto another cactus. This is done because the old man has very weak roots which are not suited to a non-desert climate. Many cacti are treated in this way, with very good results. This cactus should be kept warmer in winter than most other cacti. About 54° F. is fine. Keep rather dry.

## Chamaedorea
## (Parlor Palm, Neanthe Palm) ▶

Since most palms soon become too big for a normal room, people often look for a small palm that will stay small. This quality has been found in *Chamaedorea elegans* 'Bella'. It is seldom higher than 3 feet and has gracefully bending leaves. A speciality of this palm is that it flowers so easily. I'm sorry you cannot see this in my photograph, but the blooms look like strings with small yellow bulbs along them.
Palms are usually grown in small but high pots. The best soil is loam with rotten manure and sand. Good rainage is required. Propagation is by seed, which is sown in warm soil.

## Chamaerops (European Fan Palm) ▶▶

The European Fan Palm from the Mediterranean coast is also a small palm, but it has a completely different appearance. The leaves are very stiff and grow in the shape of a fan. The height is reasonable, to 3 feet, but older plants grow rather broad. A very good place for the plant is in a cool hall if there is sufficient light. The best thing to do with your Fan Palm is to put it outside in summer, but not in direct sunshine. Give it plenty of water and some plant food. In the winter you can keep the palm very dry, provided it is kept cool. Even a little bit of frost won't harm the plant.
Propagation is by seed.

## Clerodendron (Glory Bower) ▶

This Glory Bower vine can climb as high as 12 feet in a heated greenhouse. Best know is *Clerodendron thomsonae* from Africa.
In tropical weather it is possible to keep the plant outside. In most cases, however, a greenhouse is better. From November to January a rest period is necessary; the temperature should then fall to 54–60° F. and watering should be diminished. Most leaves will disappear during this period. In the beginning of February cut the plant back sharply, repot, and bring the temperature back to 68° F.
Propagating is from young shoots; warmth is necessary for rooting.

## Cleyera (Sakaki) ▶▶

*Cleyera japonica* (syn. *Eurya japonica*) is in most cases regarded as an ordinary *Ficus*. But there is a big difference. This plant prefers a *cool* room, whereas the *Ficus* requires warmth for healthy growing. The most common variety is called 'Tricolor' and its leaves are lighter on the edges, sometimes even pinkish.
If you take good care of your *Cleyera* you may see the sweet swelling, yellowish-white flowers. Use this plant in company with other decorative foliage plants that like a cool climate; winter temperature should be 50–54° F.
Propagation is by cuttings, but it is difficult and takes a long time.

# Conophytum (Coneplant) ▶

These small succulent plants resemble *Lithops* or Living Stones. The difference is that *Conophyta* have much smaller bodies or *corpuscula*. They consist of leaves grown together.

As you can see in the picture, *Conophytum* makes beautiful flowers, appearing freely. Compared with the size of the plant itself they are enormous.

Most species start growing only in the summer. Give them hardly any water before that time, and when growth has stopped, keep them dry again. Winter temperature should be somewhere around 60° F.

# Cryptanthus (Earth Stars) ▶▶

We cultivate most bromeliads for their interesting flowers, but this is not the case with *Cryptanthus*. The tiny rosettes are kept mainly for their fascinating colors and patterns. Flowers, as shown in the photograph, are not shiny. Four interesting species are pictured here. On top is *C. bromelioides* 'Tricolor' or Rainbow Star.

At left is *C. acaulis*. In the front is a nice flowering Zebra Plant, *C. zonatus* of which a great many varieties exist. To the right is *C. lacerdae* or Silver Star.

All plants can have direct sunlight. Normal soil is suitable. Plenty of new rosettes will be formed when the plants like their environment.

# Ctenanthe ▶

*Ctenanthe* is a lesser known member of the Maranta family. These strong foliage plants are often used in plant trays and other combinations. Pictured is *C. lubbersiana* with yellow and green leaves. Another suitable species for indoor growing is *C. oppenheimiana,* whose dark green leaves with silver bands, are wine red underneath. The variety called 'Tricolor', with white, green, and silver leaves, is known as the Never Never Plant. Like all the other *Maranta, Ctenanthe* prefers moist air and a very porous soil. So add some rough peat or charcoal.

Propagating can be done by dividing plants, sometimes by cuttings.

# Cyrtomium (Holly Fern) ▶▶

These are very hardy ferns for indoor growing. Pictured is *Cyrtomium falcatum* 'Rochefordianum', a variety with fringed leaves. Sometimes this fern is also called *Polystichum*. Leaves can reach a length of more than $1\frac{1}{2}$ feet. The leathery foliage has a dark green color. For most plants this means that little light is required and this is indeed the case with *Cyrtomium*. It grows happily even under greenhouse benches.

Guard against high temperatures indoors, especially in winter. In the growing season give a good feeding and cut away old leaves.

# Dipteracanthus (Ruellia) ▶

Small tropical plants with an interesting leaf pattern and modest demands. The strongest and most common species is *Dipteracanthus makoyanus,* Monkey Plant, from Brazil (pictured). Perhaps you can see that the emerald leaf is tinted violet. *D. devosianus* resembles *D. makoyanus* but has purple stems. The plants are often used in combined plantings where they keep well as long as the atmosphere is not too dry. Now and then topping is necessary and the plants like a good feeding in summer. Propagation is done from cuttings in January or February.

# Duchesnea (Mock Strawberry) ▶▶

*Duchesnea indica* (also called *Fragaria indica*) is sometimes called the indoor strawberry. As you can see in the picture, strawberry-like fruits are produced, but they only serve show purposes and are not edible.
Florists often train these fruit-bearing plants to a circle like the one in the photograph. Yellowish flowers precede the fruits. You can put the plant in an airy window or put it in your garden. As the plants are rather hardy, you can even leave them outside during the winter in southern regions. The old plant will probably die, but young shoots can survive and they produce new plants next season. You can also propagate the plants from fruits, sown in April.

# Dracaena ▶

Dracaenas are the most enduring and resistant houseplants of all. When you first have them in your room, they do not always give you that impression, but once they are accustomed to their environment, they last a long time.
*D. marginata* (pictured) looks delicate, but in my experience is the strongest of all. When it grows older it will form a long stalk with a bunch of leaves at the top. In fact, that is the way most *Dracaena* grow. Some species have a lot of yellow in their leaves, which means they require strong light. Of course completely green ones can endure the darkest places.
Propagating can be done from seed as well as from stem pieces.

# Echinocactus (Gold Ball Cactus) ▶▶

Years ago, many species belonged to *Echinocactus,* but nowadays it is a very poor genus with only a few. Best known is *Echinocactus grusonii* of which you see a 3 year-old specimen in the picture. It is healthy and has a wonderful color, but flowers infrequently. These plants can grow very old, reaching enormous proportions. To keep your Gold Ball Cactus healthy, keep it cool in the winter (about 50° F.) and give it hardly any water. Repot in the spring; pots should not be too small.

# Echinocereus (Hedgehog Cactus) ►

These cacti have columnar or ramified bodies and extraordinarily big flowers. Some are green, others have white-haired bodies or are closely grown with prickles. You can grow the green ones outside in summer. Just put the pots in a sunny place and forget them. They will produce a great many flowers.

The other species are grown inside, preferably in a cactus house. In winter keep them cold and don't give any water.

Well-known species include *E. baileyi,* with masses of purple flowers; *E. dasyacanthus,* which has a pink to gray body and yellow flowers and is called Rainbow Cactus; and *E. pectinatus,* which is very neatly thorned in rows, and whose flowers are purple.

# Episcia (Flame Violet) ►►

Very nice, tiny leaf plants that like warmth and humid air. There are a lot of interesting varieties and all of them have beautifully colored leaves.

Best known is *E. cupreata* (pictured), with copper-toned leaves, that are hairy and wrinkly with a bright stripe in the middle. Varieties like 'Emerald Queen' and 'Viridifolia' have a more greenish leaf. Flowers are always scarlet. *E. lilacina* is a creeper which produces green or red offshoots, and is also very variable in its leaf color.

Use flat pots and a very porous soil to which rough peat or charcoal is added. Minimum temperature in winter is 65° F. Propagation is by cuttings.

# Erica (Heather) ► VRES

Of course you can grow most heathers in the garden, even in northern zones. But there are a few species that are typical potted plants. Best known is *Erica gracilis* (pictured) from South Africa, with small flowers varying from white to red. The plant flowers from September, until spring. There are also two hybrids commonly cultivated: the winter-flowering *E. x hyemalis,* with bigger flowers in trusses, whose colors range from red to white, and *E. x wilmorei* a spring-flowering plant with inch-long, red leaves with green edging.

All heathers should be kept as cool as possible, with a minimum winter temperature of 45° F. Water well in summer and use lime-free soil for potting.

# Espostoa (Peruvian Old Man) ►►

Like the longer-haired *Cephalocereus senilis* (see page 22) this cactus has adapted itself to special circumstances. The hairs are needed to protect the plant from the hot sun in its natural habitat. In Peru, where it orginates, it can grow to 12 feet high, and its white flowers bloom at night. Cultivated as a houseplant it will be much smaller and flowers will seldom appear. Perhaps the most beautiful species is the small *Espostoa nana* (pictured). In summer, air should be moist; in winter, keep dry like other cacti, but warmer, about 54° F.

# Euonymus (Euonymus) ▶ BRSL

Primarily grown as garden plants, these can be transformed into houseplants for cool rooms. Two similar species are popular. *E. fortunei* 'Winter Creeper' often has roots on its shoots, while *E. japonicus* (Evergreen Euonymus) does not. For the rest, both exist in forms with variegated leaves, e.g. 'Argenteovariegatus', white striped; 'Aureomarginatus', with a yellow margin, and others. To have success with these plants you should put them outside in summer and feed well. In winter they should be kept as cool as possible.

Propagate in August—October easily, from cuttings.

# Exacum (Persian Violet) ▶▶

The pretty, yellow-eyed flowers adorn *Exacum affine,* a member of the Gentian family. Florists cultivate this biennial from the Socotra Islands by sowing in February in a warm greenhouse, and seedlings are put 6 together in pots and sold beginning in July, and throughout the summer.

If you want to have as much pleasure from these plants as possible, give them a light, but not a sunny place. Keep the window open so that fresh air is provided, or put the plants outside. Feed now and then.

# Faucaria (Tiger Jaws) ▶

The best-known species is *F. tigrina,* called Tiger Jaws because the thick, opposed leaves are keeled and equipped with long teeth. With some imagination you could picture the unpleasant sight of a gaping jaw. The other species have more or less the same appearance. Flowers are in all cases yellow or orange and resemble those of most *Mesembryanthemum* family members.

Like succulents, this plant should be kept dry and cool in winter, repotted in spring, and put in a sunny place in the summer. Flowering does not start until September and then only with sufficient sunlight. Rain keeps the flowers closed.

Propagation is from seed.

# Ferocactus (Barrel Cactus) ▶▶

These cacti are familiar to those who know the American Southwest or Mexico. Old specimen can easily reach a height of 12 feet and the bodies, round or barrel-shaped in smaller plants, become columnar. *Ferocactus* thorns are among the hardest known. The thorns are commonly of two types: flat and thick, bent like a fishhook at the top or thinner finer, prickles.

In the picture this difference in thorns is not very striking; notice the interesting color of some thorns, a characteristic feature of the Barrel Cactus.

Cultivate in rich, loamy soil, grafted (left) or on their own roots. Keep cool and dry in winter and propagate from seed.

# Gardenia (Gardenia) ▶

These very popular plants, are grown for their flowers, and are often worn as corsages. The smell of the white, waxy flowers is heavenly. 'Belmont' or 'Hadley' is the variety that is commercially grown. *Gardenia jasminoides* 'Fortuniana' is available as a houseplant. In most zones you can grow it outside in summer, as long as there is sun, warmth, and moisture. Night temperatures, however, should not exceed 60–62° F., or buds will not form. In winter a rest period should be given. Water sparingly and keep at 54–60° F.
Older plants can be cut back or propagated in spring by cuttings.

# Gasteria (Gasteria) ▶▶

In the picture you see some species of *Gasteria,* a succulent tribe of the Lily family. The leaves are always fleshy and serve to retain water for dry periods. From this fact you might conclude that overwatering, especially in winter, is the easiest way to kill them. Though true to some extent, they are very hardy plants and most species are absolutely resistant to any ill-treatment. At left you see *G. caespitosa* or Pencil Leaf, at the back is *G. maculata,* spotted Gasteria, from the Cape of Good Hope. Scarlet flowers may be produced on long stems, but only if you keep the plants cool and relatively dry in winter.

# Grevillea (Silk Oak) ▶

You may be surprised to learn that this fern-like houseplant, is actually a tree from western Australia, able to reach 60 feet with ease. For a time you can keep it in the room, but it will soon become stalky. If you try to pinch the top in order to get side shoots, you will merely see a new top growth as the result. Flowers appear only on mature trees. So this is, in fact, a kind of Bonsai-growing, although it is not accepted as such.
The silk oak can be put outside during summer and likes a winter temperature of 40° F. Don't feed too much.
Propagation is done from imported seeds.

# Guzmania (Guzmania) ▶▶

This is a lesser-known genus of Bromeliad cultivated for indoor growing. The almost 120 species grow all over South and Central America. In moist rain forests they grow on trees and also in the earth. Pictured is *Guzmania lingulata* major, Scarlet Star, from Colombia. *G. lingulata* 'minor' called Orange Star, is also well known. It has smaller rosettes with many leaves.
Like most bromeliads, *Guzmania* should be cultivated in a warm greenhouse. But when a flower bud is opening, the plant can be put in the room for decorative purposes and stay there for months. Afterwards the old rosette dies and propagating should be done from young plants that appear at the base.

# Gymnocalycium (Plaid Cactus) ▶

*Gymnocalycia* are among the easiest flowering cacti. Only the biggest errors in cultivation will harm them. The many species, some of which are pictured, are small spheres in colored green, almost black, brownish, or absolutely red. The red one, a form of *G. mihanovichii var. friederichii* was first cultivated in Japan in 1941. Because there is no chlorophyl in the body, it only grows when grafted. A yellow cultivar was orginated in 1970. Many people think the little colored spheres are flowers, but actually they are the cacti themselves.
All species should be kept cool and dry in winter.

# Haworthia (Haworthia) ▶▶

These interesting, easy-to-cultivate succulent plants have fleshy leaves which grow in rosettes. The surface is often strikingly arrayed with bright dots or lines. Pictured left to right are: *H. tortuosa* with leaves grouped in a spiral; *H. turgida* (front) with windows at the top of the leaves; *H. reinwardtii* (back) growing straight upward; and *H. fasciata,* best-known, with dots forming lines on the leaves. From three plants you can see flower stems running out of the picture. They are extremely long and carry small pink, red, or orange flowers. The plants should be kept in well-drained pots, with a minium temperature of 50° F. in winter.

# Howeia (Kentia Palm) ▶

The specimen of *Howeia forsteriana,* Paradise Palm, that you see in the red high-hat is only a very young one. Older palms may have leaves 7 feet long. The growth is upright, whereas *H. belmoreana,* Sentry Palm, grows arching.
Both species are very hardy and cultivation is easy. Pots must be small and deep, the soil loamy. Put the plants outside in summer when the weather is nice or when it is raining gently. Now and then soak the pots in water to which a nutrient is added. Winter temperature for the Sentry Palm is not under 60° F., but the Paradise Palm endures 50° F. Propagation is done from seed.

# Ixora (Flame-of-the-Woods) ▶▶

This is a warmth-loving tropical plant from Indonesia. Actually, it is a greenhouse plant but nevertheless growers offer it as an indoor plant.
Hybrids of *I. coccinea* are cultivated. They have scarlet, orange-red, or salmon red flowers. The soil must be loamy and pots should not be too big. In the room, spray as often as possible to humidify the air. In winter temperature should be 60° F. and little water is required. Propagation is done from cuttings at any time of the year. Soil temperature should be 75–85° F.

# Kalanchoë (Kalanchoë) ▶

Some species of *Kalanchoë* were in former times referred to as *Bryophyllum,* literally, brood-leaf, which refers to the fact that the plants have little plants formed on the leaves. They fall off and automatically become new plants, so propagation is very easy and very cheap.

Pictured is *K. daigremontiana,* often called Good Luck Plant, which has tiny plants all along the leaf edges, and in front of it, *K. tubiflora,* with young plants at the top of the cylindrical leaves. Although most succulent plants are kept more or less dry, *Kalanchoë* should be fairly moist all the year round. Give a little rest in winter, but don't lower the temperature too much. Propagation takes care of itself.

# Lantana (Lantana) ▶▶

This small shrubby plant from the West Indies is often used as a bedding plant and in the tropics it can be found growing wild. Sometimes florists bring hybrids for use as houseplants. They have yellow, orange, or salmon red flowers. In a sunny windowsill these *Lantana camara-hybrids* will grow and bloom well, provided that you feed them every fortnight and take away the old flowers. At the end of the season you can store the old plants at a temperature of 46–50°F. and take cuttings in January.

# Laurus (Laurel Sweet Bay) ▶

The real *Laurus nobilis,* a shrub that grows up to 30 feet in subtropic regions, is often trimmed to pyramidal or columnar shapes, or sold as a standard. But the plant is just as pretty when you leave it uncut and only take away the branches that are really too long. This will give you more than enough leaves for kitchen use! The best thing you can do is put your Sweet Bay in a nice tub and place it in the sun in summer. During the winter you have to find it a light, but above all things, cool place (about 34–44° F.) and only give it a little water.
Cuttings can be taken in spring and in autumn.

# Liripope (Lily Turf) ▶▶

This grass-like plant, member of the Lily family, resembles the *Ophiopogon* (page 44), except for its bright violet flowers. Pictured is the form 'Variegata' with yellow-striped leaves. Plants are easy to grow, especially when you put them in the garden in the summer in a lightly shaded place. In winter, temperature should be around 60° F. Give a rich compost, consisting of loam and peat, and feed well during the growing period.
Propagation is done by division.

# Lithops (Living Stones) ▶

Growing *Lithops* in a sunny room, or even better, in a greenhouse is convenient since the plants take little room. Young plants have a split in the middle (shown front right); when they grow older two new bodies (which are actually very fat leaves) appear in the opening (shown at back). The flowers are relatively large and resemble those of all *Mesembryanthemaceae* (front left).
*Lithops* should be kept warm and sunny in summer, but during the winter rest period no water should be given and temperatures should be around 50° F.

# Lobivia (Cob Cactus) ▶▶

This group of spherical cacti, grows in northern Argentina and Bolivia. The name is an anagram of the latter country. Plants are easy to cultivate and can be recommended to any beginner who wants to see an abundance of flowers. Some species never form sprouts; others do very easily (front), and in a few years will have formed clusters.
*Lobivia* species like soil a bit moister than most other cacti and hence the soil should contain a bit more humus or peat. Most species grow well on their own roots, some do better when grafted onto *Eriocereus jusbertii*. In winter the temperature should fall to 40–50° F and no water should be added.

# Lycaste ▶

*Lycaste* species are easily cultivated orchids, *L. skinneri* (white to pink flowers in the winter) and *L. cruenta* (orange-yellow flowers in March—May) can be kept in a rather cool room, preferably a window facing east. Potting soil can be a mixture of fern roots, sphagnum moss, and leaf mold. In June new shoots will develop and this is the best time to repot. In summer, plants can be kept in a cold frame. Growth will continue in autumn and the orchid needs plenty of water in a lightly heated room. After flowering a rest period is given with hardly any water.

# Mammillaria (Pin Cushion Cactus) ▶▶

There are hundreds and hundreds of different *Mammillaria* species, most of them originating in Mexico. Flowers appear very abundantly, in most cases they are small and grouped in a circle around the top of the plant. Most species have spherical bodies; others form columns or sprout into numerous new bodies. The groups of spines are regularly placed as are the thorns, which often have nice colors. The flowers are succeeded by colored fruits.
Nearly all kinds like a mineral soil, to which a little humus has been added.
In winter the temperature must fall to 40–50° F.

# Medinilla (Rose Grape) ▶▶

The strange *Medinilla magnifica* from the Philippines with angled woody branches and leathery leaves with ivory lines is certainly not an easy houseplant. In the first place it grows rather big, certainly too large for a windowsill. Secondly, the plant loves moist air, especially in winter. So the best environment is a greenhouse and if you don't have one, see that the air is very moist. The rest period is November–February, when less water is given and temperature falls to 60° F. Flower buds should be visible before you give more water and raise the temperature.
Propagation from cuttings, but this is not easy.

# Microcoelum (Dwarf Cocos Palm) ▶

This little palm is often called Cocos, because of the resemblance of its leaf with the big *Cocos nucifera*. But the correct name of the pictured plant is *Microcoelum weddelianum,* although it is often referred to in America as *Syagrus weddelliana*. That's a lot of names for such a small plant, not much bigger than 3 feet high, usually much smaller. Keep this palm warm, never under 65° F. Cultivate in small but deep palm pots.
Propagating is done from imported seed that is first softened in warm water. Germinating temperature is 75–85° F.

# Neoregelia (Fingernail Plant) ▶▶

This is a typical showplant, used for filling in plantings for offices, houses, etc. The florist will grow it for you, until tiny blue flowers appear in the heart of the plant. These flowers do not grow taller; they remain tucked away in the center. The appeal of this plant lies mainly in its striking leaf colors.
It does not matter so much whether you keep this bromeliad where it's light or dark, warm or cool. After having flowered, the rosette slowly dies away. This, however, takes several months, sometimes even longer. In the meantime young plants will be found at the base. You can take them for propagation.

# Nertera (Coral Bead Plant) ▶

This creeping groundcover from high, cold, and wet rocks in New Zealand, the Andes, and Cape Horn is cultivated as an indoor plant by flower growers all over the world.
Sowing is done in February–March, warm. For the first year the plants are kept in a cold frame, at temperatures just above frost level. The following year with some bottom heat, the plants will bloom with small, greenish flowers. The pollen must be distributed with a small brush or something of the kind. Later the translucent, orange fruit will develop. Keep the temperature low and moisture high.

# Odontoglossum ▶

*Odontoglossum* species are among the easiest orchids to grow indoors. At least according to my experience, *O. bictoniense* (pictured), *O. grande* (the popular Tiger Orchid), *O. insleayi, O. miltonia laevis, O. pulchellum* (called Lily of the Valley Orchid), *O. rossii,* and *O. schlieperianum* can be grown all year round in a normally heated room. The reason is that these orchids really like relatively dry air. A window facing east is the best you can have. The *Odontoglossum* species are potted in a mixture of fern roots, peat, and leaf mold. Drain well with pot-pieces. In summer, fresh air is very good and you may water freely. Winter temperature (during the period after flowering) in 48° F; give no water.

# Ophiopogon (Lily Turf) ▶▶

*Ophiopogon* species are grass-like members of the Lily family that greatly resembles *Liriope* (see page 38). The main difference is that *Ophiopogon's* flowers are white. Very common is *O. jaburan,* White Lily Turf, (pictured). There is also another species, called *O. japonicus,* which forms shoots at its base and has very small leaves, which are close together. Flowers don't grow above the height of the leaves. Its common name is Dwarf Lily Turf.
Both plants can be placed outside in summer. Winter temperature need not be higher than 60° F.
Propagation through dividing.

# Opuntia (Prickly-pears) ▶ NOPÁL

The easy-to-grow *Opuntia* cacti have different popular names, like Bunny Ears, Paperspiner and Beavertail. They are very common indeed. In southern regions you can grow them outside and some *Opuntia* will even stand New York frosts!
There is one tricky thing that you find with all Prickly-pears: in addition to their bigger thorns, they have small fish-hooked thorns, called glochides. When you touch the plant, these tiny prickles immediately break off and stay in your fingers.
*Opuntia* species can have very different shapes, some of which are shown in the picture. Keep them cool in winter, otherwise they will not flower.

# Pachyphytum (Moonstones) ▶▶

These succulent plants look very much like *Echeveria*. In fact, crossings between the two genera have been made and named x *Pachyveria*. In the picture you see two typical specimens (left is *P. hookeri*, right is *P. weinbergii*) with their thick, almost round leaves in rosettes. Sometimes the leaves have an egg form (e.g. *P. oviferum*). Most plants flower easily, as long as you keep them cool and dry in the winter season and use pots that are spacious enough. In summer you may put them in a sunny window. Red flowers appear in late spring.
The leaves, which come off easily, can be propagated after having been dried a few days.

*PELARGONIE*

# Pelargonium (Geranium) ► *KAKOS*

There are a lot of different geraniums, some of which you can grow in the garden; others are more suitable for indoor cultivation. In the white pot is a garden geranium or *Zonale-hybrid*. The leaves have dark brown edges. In the black pot a *Peltatum-hybrid* or hanging geranium is shown. Both plants can also be used outside in summer. In the background is *P. radens* or Crawfoot Geranium. It has musty-scented, feathery leaves. There are many other varieties including nutmeg, rose, peppermint, and apple geraniums. Grow them in a light and airy environment, take cuttings in August and keep these in a cool greenhouse or room during winter. Next year you can grow them to mature plants.

# Persea (Avocado Plant) ►►

The *Persea americana* is a big tree, about 60 feet high, originating in tropical America. The fruits have a delicate taste and are therefore cultivated in nearly all tropical climates. When the fruit is eaten, a large stone is left, which you can then put into a pot with sandy earth. If you keep it wet, a new avocado plant will germinate. I doubt whether you will ever see fruits on this *Ficus*-like foliage plant, but it can stay a long time in your room. If the air is too dry, the bottom leaves will soon drop.

# Phoenix (Date Palm) ►

These hardy, perhaps a bit old-fashioned palms for indoors, were much cultivated in the twenties. They may make comeback. In the picture you see *Phoenix canariensis*, a rather stiff, upright-growing palm that can be kept very cool. In tropical regions it is often grown for outdoor decoration.
Completely different, milder looking, is *P. roebelinii* or Pigmy Date Palm. It resembles the *Microcoelum* or Cocos Palm (cover, page 42) a bit, but the leaf feathers are farther apart and grow horizontally. It likes a higher temperature.
Cultivate in deep pots or tubs, put them outside when a soft rain falls in summer.

# Pisonia (Birdcatcher Tree) ►►

This *Ficus*-like foliage plant, in America often (falsely) referred to as *Heimerliodendron,* has seed pods covered with a sweet gum which attract birds. You probably won't see this phenomenon — which is normal in New Zealand — in your own room, but *Pisonia umbellifera* 'Variegata' is an attractive foliage plant when it is young and like the variegated *Ficus*, it can be grown in a warm room. The room should not be too dark, because the white parts of the leaves do not take part in photosynthesis and the receptive surface therefore is limited. Temperature must not fall in winter. Propagation from cuttings, kept at a soil temperature of 80°F.

# Plumbago (Cape Plumbago) ▶

*Plumbago auriculata,* the presently accepted name, was formerly known as *P. capensis* This shrub from South Africa has long, almost climbing shoots that are sometimes led around an iron wire, just as *Stephanotis.* The color of the flowers is a magnificent light blue. It likes a sunny, warm place in the summer, perhaps in a sheltered garden or patio. In the autumn, the plants should be stored for the winter period in a cool place. Best is a greenhouse, but a cool room can also provide suitable conditions Its temperature is kept at 35–48° F.
Propagation from cuttings in the winter.

# Polyscias (Polyscias) ▶▶

Cultivated as garden plants in the tropics. *Polyscias* can be grown in a warm room or, preferably, in greenhouses.
Pictured is *Polyscias guilfoylei* 'Victoria' or Lace Aralia, densely growing with white edged, fern-like leaves. Resembling a fern even more is *P. fruticosa,* the Ming Aralia with 3 to 4 times pinnated leaves. *P. balfouriana* 'Pennockii', Balfour Aralia, has complete round leaves, which grow in groups of three. They have a creamy white pattern.
In southern regions with moist air, the plant can grow outside in summer. Temperature 70° F. Feed well.
Propagate by cuttings.

# Pseuderanthemum ▶

These tropical foliage plants are very attractive in a warm, shaded greenhouse. They also grow indoors, preferably in tubs or planted together with other plants.
Pictured is *Pseuderanthemum atropurpureum* 'Tricolor', which has white flowers with purple dots. *P. sinuatum* has olive green and gray linear leaves and the Chocolate Plant, *P. alatum,* whose copper brown papery leaves are blotched silver along the midrib.
Since young plants are the most beautiful, take cuttings now and then and let them root at 75° F.

GRANÁTOVÉ JABLÍČKO
# Punica (Pomegranate) ▶▶

The pomegranata originates in western and southern Asia. The 6–12 foot high tree bear round fruits with a calyx on top. Fruit flesh is edible and gives a delightful juice.
The best way to keep a pomegranate is to place it in a tub (not too big) and keep it in the garden in summer. The farther south you live, the better the *Punica* will grow. Soil consists of old loam with rotted manure and sand.
Winter temperatures should be kept frost-free, but as low as possible (36–42° F.) This is to prevent premature sprouting. Most commonly grown is *P. granatum* 'Nana' (pictured) which never exceeds 5 feet. Propagate from cuttings in March.

# Rhoeo (Moses-in-the-Cradle) ▶    ◖❙ ◊◊ 🖌 🖌 **K**

This plant looks like a bromeliad, but it belongs to the *Commelina* family, so it is related to *Tradescantia* and so on. The leaves form a rosette, but the strange flowers do not appear from the plant's middle. Rather they are enclosed in boat-shaped bracts, hence the common name. *Rhoeo spathacea* which comes from Mexico, has metallic green leaves with purple undersides. Much nicer is *Rhoeo spathacea* 'Vittata' (pictured) with yellow stripes.
Propagate from shoots, which are formed after the top has been pinched out.

# Rosa (Rose) ▶▶ RŮŽE    ☼❙ ◊◊🖌 **K**

Dwarf shrub roses can be grown indoors as well as outside and you will quite often see them potted in florist shops. There are dozens of varieties of miniature, dwarf, or fairy roses. The types offered for indoor growing are exactly the same as the outdoor miniatures, so when you are fed up with them, place the shrubs in the garden, with or without their pots.
Following nature's seasons, the baby roses most be kept cool in winter. The leaves may fall off. In spring, cut the shoots back and repot.

# Scindapsus (Satin Pothos) ▶    ◖❙ ◊◊🖌 **A**

There has been some name-changing in this genus and as a result the Devil's Ivy, formerly *Scindapsus aureus,* is now called *Rhaphidophora*. Due to the name-changing, the only houseplant left under this name is *Scindapsus pictus* from Indonesia, of which the form 'Argyraeus', with silver blotches on a greenish velvet fond, is pictured here.
This plant can hang from a basket or climb a wall in any heated room, where it can grow as far as 12 feet from the window. Propagating is easily done through cuttings which root in a heated soil.

# Sedum (Sedum) ▶▶ ROZCHODNÍK    ☼❙ ◊. **K**

There are many interesting and easy-to-grow *Sedums,* most of them with thick, fleshy leaves which clearly exhibit the succulent nature. In the picture (left) is a species with more or less 'normal' leaves: *Sedum sieboldii,* the October plant, which has a hanging tendency and can be grown in baskets. The tall plant in the back is *S. griseum* from Mexico, a very strong fast-growing plant with white flowers. Front right is *S. rubrotinctum* or Christmas Cheers.
All Sedums should be kept warm and sunny in summer, but cool and dry during winter. Temperature 42–50° F.
Propagate from cuttings.

# Selaginella (Selaginella) ▶

VRANEČEK

Selaginella species are fern-allied plants which grow in moist rain forests of tropical zones; some species are found in Mexico and Texas as well. Several are cultivated as houseplants, and sold by florists. The best thing is to pot them together with other plants so that sufficient moisture is present.

In the photograph is (back) Selaginella martensii 'Watsoniana', one of the prettiest species. Front left is the moss-like S. apoda, and to the right S. kraussiana, very common variety called Irish Moss.

Temperatures should be kept around 50–68° F., summer and winter. Propagate by dividing.

# Sempervivum (Houseleek) ▶▶ NETŘESK

Sempervivum species are interesting succulent plants with leaves in rosettes. They are suitable for growing indoors and outdoors as well. The plants are very resistant to drought. According to folktale, common Houseleek is said to protect houses against cholera and lightning, and it was often grown on farmhouse roofs for this purpose. In the picture you see a collection of Houseleeks, the common S. tectorum or Hen-and-Chickens in front, a flower-stalk at the back and a smaller species right at the back. Also well known is S. arachnoideum, the Cobweb Houseleek whose tiny rosettes appear to be covered with silver cobwebs. Keep these plants in a spot as sunny and as cold as possible.

# Senecio (Groundsel) ▶ STARČEK

Senecio includes very different species, some non-succulent plants, most others succulent. Best known is the Cineraria, S. cruentus, which occurs in a great many colors. Pictured are a succulent and a half-succulent species. At left is the interesting and easy-to-grow succulent Senecio herreianus, with absolutely round leaves. To the right is S. macroglossus 'Variegatus', with thick, fleshy leaves. It resembles the green-leaved German Ivy, called S. mikanioides.

Keep the plants dry, especially in winter, when a lower temperature should also be given.

Propagation is very easy from cuttings.

# Setcreasea (Purple Heart) ▶▶

This plant, often called Tradescantia, has flowers and leaves of nearly the same shade. It is a rare plant; the lilac colored one is especially so. The plant originates from Mexico, where temperatures can be high, but in certain cases, it withstands frost too. So in southern zones you can try to plant it outside, ideally in front of a wall facing south. Indoors, see that the Setcreasea purpurea gets as much light as possible. This will strengthen the colors. Combine with other colorful foliage plants to obtain best effects.

Cuttings root very easily which is an advantage, since young plants are more attractive.

# Skimmia (Skimmia) ▶

This small shrub, also grown in the garden, is often sold as a houseplant because of its nice fruit. Don't confuse it with the *Ardisia* on page 16.
*Skimmia japonica* is dioecious, which means that there are male plants (often called *S. fragrans*) and female plants (called *S. oblata*). It is, of course, only the female plants that bear the nice red fruit. They are not completely ripe in the picture.
If the plant is kept in a cool room, the fruit will last for perhaps 6 months. Give plenty of water. Place outside the following summer. To obtain fruit again, a male plant should be within a few feet of the female.

# Sonerila (Sonerila) ▶▶

*Sonerila* are among the most beautiful foliage plants for the warm greenhouse. Indoors you may keep them alive for a while, but in most cases they will go into shock and look faint.
Most cultivated is *Sonerila margaritacea* 'Argentea' (pictured), a lovely variegated plant with pink flowers. The leaves are very sensitive to water, so never spray them overhead or will result stains. Temperature should never fall below 68° F.
Since only young plants are beautiful, take cuttings every February. They root easily in 85° F. soil.

# Spathiphyllum (Spathe Flower) ▶

The Spathe Flower has very white flowers indeed. The bloom that is visible is actually the spathe or sheathing around the flowers which are themselves hardly visible. The whole looks like a white Flamingo Plant.
Two species are cultivated as houseplants: *S. floribundum* (pictured) and *S. patinii*. They are very much alike. Culture is most successful in a warm greenhouse where the air is moist. But Spathe Flowers will also bloom in a heated room.
Keep a temperature of about 68–72° F., minimum in winter 58–62° F. Cut flowers stay fresh in water for a long time.
Propagate from seed or by division.

# Stapelia (Carrion Flower) ▶▶

There are numerous carrion plants so called because they attract certain flies by the awful smell of their flowers. This deceit is necessary for pollenation. *Stapelia variegata* is the easiest one to cultivate. The flowers have a strong resemblance to crosses of knighthood. Stems are succulent and leafless.
Cultivation indoors is fairly easy in well-drained pots, filled 1/3 with potsherds. The soil should be very porous. Sun must be shaded at midday. Always be very careful with water, especially in winter, when watering is hardly necessary and temperatures are kept between 42–54° F.
Propagate from cuttings; let them dry first.

# Stenotaphrum
# (St. Augustine Grass) ▶

The common green variety of this grass, which originates in tropical America, is often grown as a lawn grass in those regions and in the American South. In the picture the variegated form, *Stenotaphrum secundatum* 'Variegatum' is a plant that is sometimes offered for indoor growing. It is most effectively grown in a hanging basket, together with other hanging plants. Any temperature between 40° and 75° F. is satisfactory, and the grass takes sun or shade as it comes.

Young plants are formed on the hanging shoots, so it is easy to take cuttings.

*PTÁČEK Z RÁJE*

# Strelitzia (Bird of Paradise) ▶▶

Because of their beautiful flowers, these plants are often cultivated for cutting purposes. In subtropical regions the plants will grow outdoors, as long as frosts are not too heavy. For cultivation indoors or in a greenhouse, use large pots or tubs filled with a mixture of loamy soil, leaf mold, well-rotted manure, and some sand. Take care that the fleshy roots are not damaged.

In summer the plant can use a lot of water and likes warmth. Winter temperature can be 47–57° F., but if it is lower for a short time, no damage will be done.

Propagation is from seed. *NA HAWAII JSOU I BÍLE KVETOUCÍ*

# Tetrastigma (Lizard Plant) ▶

This member of the grape family is a very attractive and fast climber for the warm greenhouse, but also for rooms that are not too dry in winter. The leaves are palmately composed and have a gray green color. White pearl-like growths often appear underneath. This is quite normal with grapes and not a disease.

Best growing temperature is 50–70° F. When it becomes too big, don't hesitate to cut back sharply.

Propagation is from cuttings, consisting of one eye and a leaf. The eye should stay above the soil, otherwise it will not form shoots. Soil temperature should be 78° F.

# Thunbergia (Clock Vine) ▶▶

*Thunbergia alata* or *Clock Vine* is only one of 200 species of *Thunbergia,* which come mainly from West Africa and India. This one is grown from seed and if you live in a warm zone, you may even grow it outside. Farther north it is a houseplant, giving masses of flowers in late spring. If you want to try yourself, order seed and sow in March on some warm soil. Plant young seedlings in pots, three together and keep them warm. At the end of May, harden them off and put sticks or iron cylinders in the pot to train the long shoots. These are annuals and should be discarded in autumn.

# Tillandsia (Tillandsia) ▶

These plants are real epiphytic bromeliads of which a great many species appear in Southern and Central America and as far north as Florida. A lot of them have no roots at all and take their moisture and food supply from the air. Among them is the astonishing Spanish Moss, *T. usneoides,* that covers whole landscapes. In a greenhouse, it can be simply hung on a nail. Pictured is the well-known *Tillandsia morreniana,* also called *T. cyanea* or *T. lindenii.* The violet flowers appear only one at a time. You can keep this plant indoors during flowering time.

# Tolmiea (Piggyback Plant) ▶▶

This simple but charming plant grows wild in the woods of America's Pacific coast. Other names are: Youth-on-Age and Mother-of-Thousands. As you can see in the photograph, a mature leaf (front right) has a young plant on its back. The weight makes the mother leaf tip over and when it touches the ground, new roots develop. If you wish, you can also take the young plants off and put them in soil.

The Piggyback Plant likes a bright place, but the temperature need not be too high. In summer you can place it outside.

# Vriesea ▶

*Vriesea* could be called the king of bromeliads, and indeed one variety, *Vriesea hieroglyphica,* with hieroglyphic patterns on its leaves, is called just that. *V. carinata,* shown at right, is called Lobster Claws, at left is *V. x poelmannii,* of which no common name is known.

Once you have a flowering *Vriesea,* the cultivation is very simple. Like a tulip bulb it can be put anywhere, as long as it is kept moist and not completely in the dark. The old rosette dies after flowering, but this takes several months. New shoots arise from the base. It takes several years for new flowers to bloom and though not easy, this can best be done in a greenhouse.

# Zantedeschia (Calla) ▶▶ DÁBLÍK

The Common Calla, also called *Richardia,* is officially *Zantedeschia aethiopica.* In South Africa it grows wild in wet meadows that dry out in summer. If you try to imitate these conditions, the culture will be easy. After they flower in June stop watering them until August. At the end of this period repot in loamy soil with old manure added. Leave the plants outside until the end of September if possible. Then take them inside a cool room or greenhouse until January, when the flowers appear and temperature can be raised. Always give a lot of water, except in the summer dormant period.

# INDEX